Vincent's COLORS

Words and pictures by
Vincent van Gogh

THE METROPOLITAN MUSEUM OF ART
New York

chronicle books · san francisco

Vincent van Gogh was an artist who loved bright colors. He was born in the Netherlands, where the rain can make things seem dark and gloomy. When he grew up, he eventually moved to the south of France, where the sun is stronger and the colors brighter.

Vincent wrote many letters to his brother, Theo. In them, he often described his dynamic, colorful paintings. Here are a few of his paintings and what he said about them.

A yellow sky with yellow sun,

a jug in squares of blue and white,

a reddish cap and orange bricks,

twelve flowers that are light on light.

Trees gray-green with a pink sky,

cypresses of a bottle-green hue,

some very yellow buttercups,

and all the ground is yellow, too.

Roses in a green vase,

a window with a green shutter,

a lady's clothes in black, black, black,

two chairs the yellow of fresh butter.

Leaves of silver turning to green,

stars sparkling, greenish, yellow, white,

a big bunch of violet irises,

and in my head a starry night.

The works of art reproduced in this book are by Vincent van Gogh (Dutch, 1853–1890). The words of this book were taken from Vincent van Gogh's letters, many of which were written in French or Dutch, to his brother, Theo. In some cases, the words were translated verbatim; in others, a free translation was used. The credits below list the letter number for the quote used on each spread. ~W. L.

LETTER 501
The Sower
Oil on canvas, 25¼ x 31¾ in., 1888
COLLECTION KRÖLLER-MÜLLER MUSEUM,
Otterlo, the Netherlands

LETTER 489
Still Life: Blue Enamel Coffeepot,
Earthenware, and Fruit
Oil on canvas, 25⅝ x 31⅞ in., 1888
PRIVATE COLLECTION

LETTER 501
The Zouave
Oil on canvas, 25⅝ x 21¼ in., 1888
VAN GOGH MUSEUM, Amsterdam
Vincent van Gogh Foundation

LETTER 526
Sunflowers
Oil on canvas, 36¼ x 28½ in., 1889
PHILADELPHIA MUSEUM OF ART
The Mr. and Mrs. Carroll S. Tyson, Jr.,
Collection, 1963

LETTER 619
Women Picking Olives
Oil on canvas, 28⅝ x 36 in., 1889-90
THE METROPOLITAN MUSEUM OF ART, New York
The Walter H. and Leonore Annenberg Collection,
Gift of Walter H. and Leonore Annenberg, 1995,
Bequest of Walter H. Annenberg, 2002   1995.535

LETTER 596
Cypresses
Oil on canvas, 36¼ x 29⅛ in., 1889
THE METROPOLITAN MUSEUM OF ART, New York
Rogers Fund, 1949   49.30

LETTER 487
View of Arles with Irises in the Foreground
Oil on canvas, 21¼ x 25⅝ in., 1888
VAN GOGH MUSEUM, Amsterdam
Vincent van Gogh Foundation

LETTER 543
The Yellow House
Oil on canvas, 28 x 36 in., 1888
VAN GOGH MUSEUM, Amsterdam
Vincent van Gogh Foundation

LETTER 684
Vase of Roses
Oil on canvas, 36⅝ x 29⅛ in., 1890
THE METROPOLITAN MUSEUM OF ART, New York
The Walter H. and Leonore Annenberg Collection,
Gift of Walter H. and Leonore Annenberg, 1993,
Bequest of Walter H. Annenberg, 2002   1993.400.5

LETTER 559
L'Arlésienne: Madame Joseph-Michel Ginoux
(Marie Julien, 1848-1911)
Oil on canvas, 36 x 29 in., 1888 or 1889
THE METROPOLITAN MUSEUM OF ART, New York
Bequest of Sam A. Lewisohn, 1951   51.112.3

LETTER 552
Tarascon Diligence
Oil on canvas, 28¼ x 36⁷⁄₁₆ in., 1888
The Henry and Rose Pearlman Foundation, Inc.
Photograph: Bruce M. White

LETTER 554
The Bedroom
Oil on canvas, 29 x 36⅜ in., 1889
THE ART INSTITUTE OF CHICAGO
Helen Birch Bartlett Memorial Collection
1926.417
Photograph: Greg Williams
Photograph © The Art Institute of Chicago

LETTER 587
Olive Orchard
Oil on canvas, 28⅝ x 36¼ in., 1889
THE METROPOLITAN MUSEUM OF ART, New York
The Walter H. and Leonore Annenberg Collection,
Gift of Walter H. and Leonore Annenberg, 1998,
Bequest of Walter H. Annenberg, 2002   1998.325.1

LETTER 499
Starry Night over the Rhone River
Oil on canvas, 28½ x 36¼ in., 1888
MUSÉE D'ORSAY, Paris
Photograph: Hervé Lewandowski
Photograph © Reúnion des Musées Nationaux / Licensed by
Art Resource, New York

LETTER 633
Irises
Oil on canvas, 29 x 36¼ in., 1890
THE METROPOLITAN MUSEUM OF ART, New York
Gift of Adele R. Levy, 1958   58.187

LETTER 614a
The Starry Night
Oil on canvas, 29 x 36¼ in., 1889
THE MUSEUM OF MODERN ART, New York
Acquired through the Lillie P. Bliss Bequest
472.1941
Photograph © The Museum of Modern Art / Licensed by
SCALA / Art Resource, New York

PAGE 2: *Self-Portrait with a Straw Hat*
Vincent van Gogh, Dutch, 1853–1890
Oil on canvas, 16 x 12¹/₂ in., probably 1887
THE METROPOLITAN MUSEUM OF ART, New York
Bequest of Miss Adelaide Milton de Groot (1876–1967), 1967 67.187.70a

PAGE 3: Detail of a page from a letter to John Russell, with a sketch of *The Sower*
Vincent van Gogh, Dutch, 1853–1890
Pen and ink on wove paper, 10⅝ x 8 in., 1888
SOLOMON R. GUGGENHEIM MUSEUM, New York
Thannhauser Collection, Gift, Justin K. Thannhauser, 1978 78.2514.19
Photograph © The Solomon R. Guggenheim Foundation

Produced by the Department of Special Publications, The Metropolitan Museum of Art.
Edited by William Lach.
Book design by Anna Raff.
Typeset in Colwell.
Manufactured in China.

In most cases, the photographs were provided by the owners of the works and are published with
their permission. Their courtesy is gratefully acknowledged. Photographs from The Metropolitan Museum of Art
were taken by The Metropolitan Museum of Art Photograph Studio.

Library of Congress Cataloging-in-Publication Data

Gogh, Vincent van, 1853–1890.
   Vincent's colors : words and pictures by Vincent van Gogh / [edited by William Lach].
     p. cm.
   ISBN 1-58839-155-8 (The Metropolitan Museum of Art) — ISBN 0-8118-5099-4
(Chronicle Books)
   1. Gogh, Vincent van, 1853–1890—Correspondence—Juvenile literature. 2. Gogh, Theo
van, 1857–1891—Correspondence—Juvenile literature. 3. Painters—Netherlands—
Correspondence—Juvenile literature. 4. Color in art—Juvenile literature. I. Lach,
William, 1968– II. Metropolitan Museum of Art (New York, N.Y.) III. Title.
   ND653.G7A3 2005
   759.9492—dc22

                                                                              2005000200

12 11 10 9 8

Chronicle Books LLC
680 Second Street, San Francisco, California 94107
www.chroniclekids.com

The Metropolitan Museum of Art
1000 Fifth Avenue, New York, New York 10028
212.570.3894
www.metmuseum.org